AF083758

A Day in the Life
ANCIENT GREECE

A Day in the Life
ANCIENT GREECE

Joanna Nadin
Santy Gutiérrez

Collins

CONTENTS

Chapter 1 Welcome to ancient Greece.....2

Map of ancient Greece................. 10

Chapter 2 At home.................... 12

A wealthy house......................22

Chapter 3 At school...................24

School – then and now.................32

Chapter 4 Food and drink 34

Food – now and then 44

Chapter 5 Fun and games...............46

The Olympic Games 56

Chapter 6 Myths and legends...........58

Glossary 68

About the author 70

About the illustrator...................72

Book chat 74

CHAPTER 1
WELCOME TO ANCIENT GREECE

Welcome to ancient Greece! My name is Jason, and I'm going to be your guide so you can experience what it was like to live about 2,500 years ago.

First of all, it's important to know that ancient Greece isn't just an old version of the modern country of Greece. In fact, it isn't actually a country at all. It's more of a collection of small cities that rule themselves and are often fighting each other. There's a LOT of fighting!

That's true, but we don't fight ALL the time! We do lots of other things too, as you'll find out!

This is my little sister, Lydia. She'll be popping up as well, although hopefully not too often.

We're from a city called **Athens**, which is a great place to live. It's warm, and we have a lot of freedom. The people here even get to vote, which is very different from another city called Sparta.

I reckon everything in Athens is better than it is in Sparta.

In Sparta, there are lots of rules. Children have to wear plain clothes, and only get to wash a few times a year. Plus, they have to sleep on beds made of rushes and thistles! Just think how scratchy that would be!

When they're seven, children leave their parents to live in 'herds'. They're made to fight to see who's the best fighter. And food is scarce so they get hungry all the time.

They are told to steal food to eat. And if they get caught, they get punished.

But they're not punished because they stole – just because they got caught!

Fact file

Sparta is where we get the English word 'spartan' from, which means 'no luxuries'.

Life in Sparta is seriously hard. It's all about fighting and war. And the two kings who reign over everything are really scary. But here in Athens we have **democracy**, which means everyone gets a say in how the country is run.

Well, everyone gets a say except women.

And poorer people.

And **enslaved** people.

And anyone under the age of 30.

Fact file

In Athens, people got to vote once a year. They wrote the name of any politician they didn't agree with on little pieces of pottery called *ostraca*. Whoever received the most votes was **exiled** for ten years. It's where we get the word 'ostracise' from, which means to leave someone out, or stay away from them.

Okay, I get it! Our democracy isn't perfect. But at least school in Athens is way cooler than in Sparta.

Weren't you going to talk about school later on?

She's right. You'll have to wait to find out how bad school in Sparta is, but be warned, it's pretty grim! Anyway, welcome to ancient Greece. I hope you have fun looking round.

MAP OF ANCIENT GREECE

Olympia

Athens

Sparta

☐ = ancient Greece

MEDITERRANEAN SEA

CHAPTER 2
AT HOME

This is where we live, with our parents, our grandparents, and our uncles and their wives and children too. It's called an **oikos** and is probably a bit different from your house. It's made of mud bricks for a start, which means it has to be repaired every few years.

None of the windows have glass in them, only shutters.

And we don't have many windows.
That makes it easier to keep the heat out in summer and the warmth in during autumn and winter.

Fact file

Although *oikos* translates as 'house', it actually means the buildings *and* all the people who lived there.

The women mostly stay upstairs and the men stay downstairs. Men and women don't even eat together!
In the middle is the courtyard. Every *oikos* has one of these. It's where everything happens – cooking, eating, and even parties!

Well, everything except washing.

Fact file

Although some wealthy ancient Greek households had bathrooms, most people had to use public baths or rivers to have a wash. They also had to use chamber pots to go to the loo, or public toilets.

Oh, you might be wondering where we sleep. Well, we don't have our own bedrooms – we just sleep in whichever room is free. Even if it's been used to cook in, earlier in the day!

And unlike Spartans, our beds are quite luxurious. They're made of wool and feathers.

Although sometimes, when it's really hot, we sleep on the roof! That's why the roofs are flat!

I don't sleep up there though. I'm too scared of falling off!

Oh, I've remembered something else! Check out the ***andron***. This is the fanciest room of all, and all our best pictures and pottery are in here. It's kept for entertaining guests, but only Dad and other men are allowed in.

That's totally unfair! Dad's not even around right now so the room is just empty.

He's off fighting the **Persians**, which is pretty scary as there are three hundred thousand of them and only seven thousand of us!

I guess it makes a change from going to war with the Spartans, though.

Fact file

Athens and Sparta were often fighting. They went to war three times in less than 80 years.

Constantly fighting with Sparta makes things a bit tricky with some of our cousins who live there!

Best not think about that. Hey, why don't you show everyone the women's quarters?

OK. This is where the women hang out. It's at the other end of the house to the *andron*, and it's where the women do all the cooking and crafts, like weaving.

The women's quarters are also where we children spend most of our time. When we're not at school, that is ...

When *you're* not at school, you mean!

Okay, okay. I'll get to that in the next chapter.

CHAPTER 3
AT SCHOOL

What's your best subject at school? Science? Oh dear. IT? Even worse! Computing hasn't even been invented yet, and we don't do any science at school. It's mostly poetry, politics and PE.

School is also expensive, and lots of parents can't afford to pay for two children to get lessons.

It's not just about money, though. School in ancient Greece is just for boys. Girls have to stay at home. Well, unless they live in Sparta.

Fact file

School in Sparta was very different to Athens. Boys started training to be elite fighters aged seven. Girls did go to school, and they also learned how to fight, with lessons in wrestling and fist fighting.

No one could persuade me to spend all day wrestling. I'd rather use a stone to wipe my bottom.

Er, you already do.

Thanks for reminding me. Luckily, Mum can read and write. She'll start teaching me next year, as well as how to cook and weave and run a household.

Fact file

Toilet paper hadn't been invented in ancient Greece. People had to use *ostraca* to wipe their bottoms. Yes, these were the same bits of stone or pottery that they also used for voting. They sometimes still had the names of their enemies written on them.

Anyway, I'd never move to Sparta. I'd have to live in **barracks** like our cousin Leon. It's a really harsh regime. He's only allowed to wear a cloak when it's freezing, and soon he'll have to play the cheese game.

> That sounds brilliant. I love cheese!

> Not this kind! The game's really violent.

Fact file

The cheese game involved two teams of boys fighting to steal cheese from a platform in the middle of a temple. The winner was the team with the most cheese at the end.

My school is pretty cool. Everyone gets to play a musical instrument – I'm learning the lyre, and my best friend Paris is learning the flute. There's loads of physical education, which I love. Keeping active is really important here in ancient Greece. We also learn poems off by heart and, best of all, we're taught how to argue properly!

You certainly do a lot of arguing!

I do not!

See what I mean?

Fact file

Children in Greece learned rhetoric, or the art of persuasion. This is a way of using words in order to get a point across clearly and effectively, for instance by using rhyme and rhythm.

This is why I like being able to escape to school! I'll keep having lessons for a while here, then I'll do some military training. I won't finish until I'm around 20 years old.

Then what?

Then I'd like to be a poet. I'd write long, solemn poems about the gods and heroes and perform them in public.

I want to be a doctor. But to do that I would have to be a man.

SCHOOL – THEN AND NOW

School has changed a lot since ancient Greek times. What differences can you see?

CHAPTER 4
FOOD AND DRINK

All this talking is making me a bit peckish. I reckon it's time to show you some of the things we eat and drink.

And perhaps have a little snack on the way?

You've guessed it!

What do you like to eat? Rice? Bananas? Too bad, neither of those exist here yet. In fact, lots of foods you know aren't eaten in ancient Greece. There are no lemons for a start, or tomatoes. They haven't reached ancient Greece yet. Nor have potatoes, so no chips either!

Fact file

Lots of foods hadn't travelled as far as ancient Greece. So, as well as lemons, rice, bananas, tomatoes and potatoes, the ancient Greeks didn't have coffee, tea or fruit juice.

We don't have sweets like yours either! That's good for our teeth, I suppose. But we do have the greatest snack of all – fresh warm bread! We eat that for *ariston*, which is what you call breakfast, with a bit of honey and some olives.

The women bake the bread every day in the women's quarters, after grinding the grain themselves.

It takes hours and is exhausting work. I'm not looking forward to that at all.

It could be worse. You could live in Sparta and have to eat this ghastly black soup!

Fact file

Black soup was a mix of beans, vinegar and an animal bone.

Yuck!

We have various sorts of vegetables, plus garlic and olives, and olive oil, of course. And a lot of fish, because we live so near the sea. I like eel the best.

This is our goat, Athena. Most homes have got a goat, so they can get milk to make cheese and yoghurt with. We sometimes eat meat, like sausages, but not very often.

And we'd never eat Athena!

Fact file

When the ancient Greeks did eat meat, it was mostly wild animals they had hunted, like hares or deer. Poorer people who lived in cities only ever had meat at festivals.

We also have many different kinds of cake to celebrate festivals, weddings and other important days. Some have goats' cheese in. The one I like the best is made of sesame seeds, olive oil and honey. Yum!

We invented putting candles on cake, too. Think of that next time you see a birthday cake with candles on!

Another thing you'd have to get used to is that we only eat twice a day. We have *ariston* at dawn, and then our main meal late afternoon.

I'm always so hungry by then, unless I've managed to get a snack, of course! Like these, which you can purchase from stalls on the street!

They're skewers with meat and vegetables on – delicious!

Thankfully Dad gave us some money for treats before he went away.

Okay, I'm full now. And I think it's time for some fun and games before our parents call us home!

FOOD – NOW AND THEN

Picture a big feast.

CHAPTER 5
FUN AND GAMES

We don't have computer games or as many toys as you do, but there's still lots of varied things to do in our spare time. The game I like best is Bronze Fly, especially when I'm doing the catching!

Fact file

To play Bronze Fly, one child would have their eyes covered and be spun around. They would then have to try to catch other children and avoid their paper whips.

Another good game is the one where we throw stones at a target. Whoever doesn't win has their eyes covered. The winner gets the honour of riding on their back!

It's nearly always me who wins. Then I get to ride around for ages until Jason touches the target with his foot.

Fact file

Another game was called Cooking Pot. One child was chosen to be the 'cooking pot'. They had their eyes covered and had to sit on the ground. The other children tried to poke them. If the cooking pot managed to touch another player with their foot, then that child became the new cooking pot.

These games are fun, but not as much fun as plays, though. Everyone in Athens loves plays. The best ones are the tragedies, especially the scary ones about the **Trojan war**.

Fact file

The ancient Greeks had two kinds of plays: tragedies, in which lots of people died, and comedies, which were full of jokes and rude bits.

Our plays are different to yours though, because the actors all wear masks. This obviously makes it easier for them to change roles. The places where they put plays on are massive as well. One can fit up to 15,000 people!

Honestly, plays are almost as exciting as the Olympic Games.

Neither have you!

How would you know? You've never even been to the Olympic Games!

True. They're only on every four years, and we weren't old enough last time. Plus, they're miles away at **Olympia**. But they do sound brilliant. They last five whole days and there's running, jumping, **chariot racing** and boxing.

chariot racing

And wrestling! Don't forget that. It's the best bit!

You're right. I love wrestling. I might even enter when I'm old enough.

Fact file

The ancient Greeks took the Olympic games really seriously. Once, when Persia invaded, the fighting had to be delayed, because the Greeks were too busy at the Olympics.

Taking part in the Olympics is another thing girls aren't allowed to do. This is unfair because the games are one of the most important things in ancient Greece. Though at least girls are allowed to watch, I suppose. Until they're married, anyway, then they have to stop going.

Fact file

All 'free' men (men who weren't enslaved) were allowed to enter the Olympics.

All this talk of fun and games is making me feel exhausted. How about we calm things down for the next chapter?

THE OLYMPIC GAMES

The first Olympic Games were held over 2,800 years ago. They're still held today and countries from around the world take part.

There are lots more events now, like swimming, diving and even skateboarding.

And we have the Paralympics which are events for athletes with disabilities.

The winter games have events like skiing, ice-skating and snowboarding.

CHAPTER 6
MYTHS AND LEGENDS

What's your bedtime routine?
Do you like to read, or have a story
read to you before you go to bed?

I bet I would, but books haven't been invented yet. Instead, we listen to the myths and legends that our parents have learned off by heart. I've heard some of those stories so many times that now I know them too.

Fact file

The ancient Greeks loved sharing and retelling their myths. These unique stories were about monsters, heroes, gods and kings who reigned long ago. In ancient Greece, people still worshipped and offered gifts to the gods and goddesses when they needed help or guidance.

Tell us a myth! The one about Icarus, who made wings and flew too close to the sun. Or Theseus and the Minotaur!

Both of those stories are way too scary. How about a **fable** instead?

Fine. Fables are good too! Why don't you tell us *The Dog and his Reflection*?

One day, a greedy dog seized a bone from a shop and ran off before anyone could catch him.

He trotted along the road to home, very pleased with his stealing technique.

On the way, he came to a bridge across a river. As he went over, he looked down into the water and saw another dog with another bone!

"Hang on a minute," he said to himself. "That bone looks just as tasty as my bone. In fact, it looks even tastier!"

The dog was so envious and greedy, he decided to jump into the water and take the other dog's bone for himself.

But when he got into the river, he couldn't see the other dog, or the other bone.

Worst of all, he couldn't see his own bone anymore either. He had lost it when he jumped in.

The greedy dog had to go home hungry and wet.

I wish we could tell you more fables.
There are loads to pick from. Check out
The Ant and the Grasshopper, or maybe one
of the myths! But be careful, as some can be
a bit scary! Like Theseus and the Minotaur!
The Minotaur was half man and half bull
and he lived in a maze called a Labyrinth!

You could read that one, if you dare. It's really scary. But I reckon that's enough from us. I'm exhausted! I hope you've had fun with us in ancient Greece. If you want to learn more after reading this book, there are lots of places you can look. Maybe you can even visit a museum to see some real-life objects from ancient Greece!

GLOSSARY

Athens one of the main cities of ancient Greece, now the capital

andron male quarters

barracks where the army live

chariot racing a contest between small, two-wheeled carts drawn by horses

democracy when adults get to vote on how a country is run

enslaved people who are made to work for someone else for no money, they are not free to do as they want

fable a story that has a message in it

moral the name for the message in a story that teaches the reader something

oikos a Greek home

Olympia a place in Greece where the first games were held, which is why we call them Olympic games

Persians people who lived in the ancient Persian empire, in the Middle East

Trojan war a war between Ancient Greece and the city of Troy

About the author

A bit about me ...

Before I became a writer, I worked in radio, television and politics. I am now the author of more than a hundred books for children and young people. I'm also a professor of creative writing and love getting young people to play around with words. I like goats, monkeys, music, cheese and ancient Greece (but not Sparta). I live in Bath.

Joanna Nadin

Why did you want to be a writer?

I started writing because my real life wasn't as exciting as the books I read when I was a child. Writing gives me a chance to go on imaginary adventures all day.

What is it like for you to write?

Writing a book is a bit like schoolwork. Sometimes it's hard and can take a lot of time. Sometimes it feels easy, flows well and I have a lot of fun.

Have you ever been to Greece?
Not yet! But I'm planning to go to Athens soon and I'm really looking forward to that.

Why did you want to write this book?
I only learned about Sparta last year and as soon as I did, I knew I wanted to learn more about ancient Greece and write about it.

What's the most interesting thing you learned while writing this book?
The most interesting fact that I learned while writing this book was that the ancient Greeks used bits of broken pottery to vote *and* to wipe their bottoms!

What do you hope readers will get from reading this book?
I hope readers will be able to picture what it's like to live for a day in ancient Greece. I hope readers see how different it is to their own life now.

If you could time-travel would you like to visit ancient Greece? Why or why not?
No – I'd be too scared I'd end up in Sparta!

What did you like to do when you were Jason's age?
When I was young like Jason, I loved board games, skipping games and riding horses.

About the illustrator

What made you want to be an illustrator?

Books have always been a big part of my life, for as long as I can remember. My parents were literature teachers and inspired me to love books and enjoy reading stories. I've always loved drawing and was fascinated by images in books.

Santy Gutiérrez

I wanted to put my own images alongside the books I read when I was growing up.

What did you like best about illustrating this book?

I love learning, and there's so much to learn in this book! I really enjoyed working on this project. I especially enjoyed designing the characters, their clothing and the settings.

Do you prefer to draw digitally or using a pencil and paper? Why?

I prefer using digital media, because it gives me the chance to correct and amend easily.

What was the most difficult part of illustrating this book?

The tricky part was bringing buildings that we are used to seeing as ruins back to life. Photographs show us the remains, but not what those buildings looked like when they were new and complete and full of people.

Do you prefer illustrating fiction or non-fiction books?

It all depends on how fun the project is! I like books where I can use my imagination. Books with adventures, fantastic creatures and original characters ... but I also enjoy drawing dinosaurs, scientific or historical non-fiction books.

What was the most interesting thing you learned while illustrating this book?

I was surprised about schools in ancient Greece and their dedication to sports and arts, as well as subjects like maths and reading. I was also surprised by the chapter about food. I enjoyed learning about ancient Greek ingredients and dishes.

Book chat

What did you know about ancient Greece before reading this book?

What's the most interesting thing you learned from reading this book?

What surprised you the most in this book?

If you could ask the siblings from the book anything, what would you ask?

Would you like to visit ancient Greece? Why or why not?

If you could ask the author anything, what would you ask?

Would you recommend this book? Why or why not?

Book challenge:

Design a poster encouraging people to visit ancient Greece on a time-travel holiday!

Published by Collins
An imprint of HarperCollins*Publishers*

The News Building
1 London Bridge Street
London SE1 9GF
UK

Macken House
39/40 Mayor Street Upper
Dublin 1
D01 C9W8
Ireland

Text © Joanna Nadin 2024
Design and illustrations © HarperCollins*Publishers* Limited 2024

10 9 8 7 6 5 4

ISBN 978-0-00-868113-5

All rights reserved. No part of this publication may be reproduced, stored in a retrieval system, or transmitted in any form by any means, electronic, mechanical, photocopying, recording or otherwise, without the prior written permission of the Publisher or a licence permitting restricted copying in the United Kingdom issued by the Copyright Licensing Agency Ltd, 5th Floor, Shackleton House, 4 Battle Bridge Lane, London SE1 2HX.

Without limiting the exclusive rights of any author, contributor or the publisher of this publication, any unauthorised use of this publication to train generative artificial intelligence (AI) technologies is expressly prohibited. HarperCollins also exercise their rights under Article 4(3) of the Digital Single Market Directive 2019/790 and expressly reserve this publication from the text and data mining exception.

British Library Cataloguing-in-Publication Data
A catalogue record for this publication is available from the British Library.

Download the teaching notes and word cards to accompany this book at:
http://littlewandle.org.uk/signupfluency/

Author: Joanna Nadin
Illustrator: Santy Gutiérrez
  (Astound Illustration Agency)
Publisher: Laura White
Product manager: Caroline Green
Series editor: Charlotte Raby
Development editor: Catherine Baker
Commissioning editor: Suzannah Ditchburn
Project manager: Emily Hooton
Copyeditor: Sally Byford
Proofreader: Catherine Dakin
Cover designer: Sarah Finan
Typesetter: 2Hoots Publishing Services Ltd
Production controller: Katharine Willard

Printed in the UK.

 MIX
Paper | Supporting responsible forestry
FSC™ C007454

This book contains FSC™ certified paper and other controlled sources to ensure responsible forest management.
For more information visit: www.harpercollins.co.uk/green

Made with responsibly sourced paper and vegetable ink
Scan to see how we are reducing our environmental impact.

Acknowledgements
The publishers gratefully acknowledge the permission granted to reproduce the copyright material in this book. Every effort has been made to trace copyright holders and to obtain their permission for the use of copyright material. The publishers will gladly receive any information enabling them to rectify any error or omission at the first opportunity.

p8 Album/Alamy, p33t Sally and Richard Greenhill/Alamy, p33c Peter Titmuss/Alamy, p33b Redsnapper/Alamy, p56 Tim Clayton – Corbis/Contributor/Getty Images, p57 PA Images/Alamy.

Get the latest Collins Big Cat news at
collins.co.uk/collinsbigcat